Baby Boomers Guide:

Finding God!

Steven L. Testerman

Baby Boomers Guide:

Finding God!

Looking for Lost Members of the
Woodstock Generation

By Steven L. Testerman

This book is dedicated to my family and friends.

I want to especially acknowledge my father Roger Testerman who passed away in 1994 – you were a hero, inspiration and an example of simple, deep Faith. And to my mother who still shows me what it is to love; to my beloved sons David and Jeff.

This book was also written for my grandsons, William, Jacob and Evan; and my granddaughter Jackie. To Joan who helped inspire me. To old friends and new - you mean the world to me!

I wrote this book with the idea that I might map the pathway that led me to Faith. Every path is different and you must walk your own way, but maybe this Guide can help you avoid some of the pitfalls, roadblocks and dead ends in life.

*Children - Don't let anyone ever tell you that there is not a God! Science will never know for sure. Follow your Heart and remember that the closer you get to Him – the more you will **know** that He exists!*

April 2015

Table of Contents

INTRODUCTION   10

THE WOODSTOCK GENERATION   12

                                                         12

BOOMERS AND GOD   16

IS THERE A GOD?   19

WHY BELIEVE IN GOD?   22

HOW MUCH FAITH?   27

QUESTIONS ABOUT OUR UNIVERSE   32

WHO CREATED OUR UNIVERSE?   36

WHICH GOD?   39

WHO IS OUR GOD?   43

GOD IN US   46

WHAT ABOUT THE BIBLE?   50

RELIGION AND BELIEFS   54

CHRISTIANITY   56

PRINCIPLES OF CHRISTIAN SALVATION   60

PRAYERS OF SALVATION   63

GOD'S PLAN   66

66

GOD'S PLAN FOR THE WORLD   69

69

WHAT'S NEXT?   71

"FOREVER YOUNG"   75

FREQUENTLY ASKED QUESTIONS   77

"HOW CAN YOU BELIEVE IN A GOD? THAT IS
SO RIDICULOUS!"   79

DOES SCIENCE DISPROVE GOD?   83

"THE IDEA OF A GOD IS PREPOSTEROUS!"   87

"AREN'T FUNDAMENTALISTS KIND OF CRAZY?"
                                                        93

"WHAT DO CHRISTIANS HAVE TO DO?"   100

WHAT IS SIN?   102

"WHY ARE CHRISTIANS SO JUDGMENTAL AND HYPOCRITICAL?"   108

"WHY DO SOME CHRISTIANS TAKE SUCH A LITERAL INTERPRETATION OF PARTS OF THE BIBLE?"   110

"WOULDN'T HEAVEN BE BORING?"   113

"I DON'T BELIEVE IN ADAM AND EVE"   115

115

"IS GOD DEAD?"   118

"WHY WOULD A GOOD GOD ALLOW BAD THINGS TO HAPPEN?"   119

ABOUT YOUR GUIDE   123

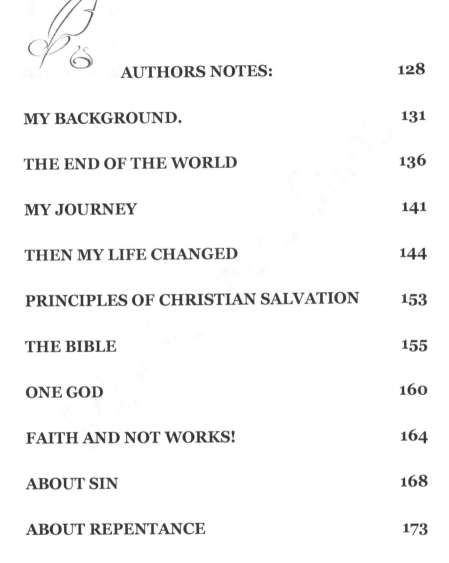

AUTHORS NOTES: 128

MY BACKGROUND.   131

THE END OF THE WORLD   136

MY JOURNEY   141

THEN MY LIFE CHANGED   144

PRINCIPLES OF CHRISTIAN SALVATION   153

THE BIBLE   155

ONE GOD   160

FAITH AND NOT WORKS!   164

ABOUT SIN   168

ABOUT REPENTANCE   173

Introduction

Baby Boomers look at the world in a bit different way than most people - we had powerful shared experiences as we dealt with the challenges of youth in a world that seemed on the brink of destruction!

In this book you will find answers to some really penetrating questions, all from a Boomer point-of-view:

- "Is there a God?"
- "Why Do Bad Things Happen?"
- "Isn't the idea of a God preposterous?"
- "How can you believe the Bible? It is Bogus!"

What renewed my interest in this deeply important topic was a conversation. Let me explain:

One of my best friends from high school told me this:

> *"I could never wrap my brain around there being a God – I just can't buy into some old guy in the clouds in a white robe - pulling our strings."*

Funny, I spent a good many years asking myself those very same questions.

Peace!

The Woodstock Generation

There are members of the "Woodstock Generation" who are Lost!

Let us try to find them.

- If you saw the Beatles on The Ed Sullivan Show
- If you know what LSMFT means
- If you cried when Old Yeller or Davy Crockett died
- If you remember the last helicopter in Saigon or when Nixon flew away from the White House in one
- If you and Jimmy Carter once had the same hairdo
- If you remember where you were when John or Bobby or Martin were assassinated

... then you may be a Boomer!

- The term Baby Boomer is actually divided into two groups:
- If you were born in '46 through '55 you are a **Core Boomer** –
  - This is the group that epitomized the Sixties.
- If you are part of the second wave born between '56 and '64
  - you are a youngster - but still allowed to read this book!

This book is written especially for the 1 in 2 Boomers who are dropouts from formal religion.

If you know a Boomer who fits this demographic then please suggest that they take a look at this *Guide*.

- There are those who think that "Religion' is a bad thing - this *Baby Boomers Guide* will try to offer up some ideas for their Spiritual contemplation.

- I want to share with you what I hope is a logical and plausible case for the existence of God - that can stand up to whatever the Scientists are saying today.
- These days there are people who want to say that God did not have to exist, or that there was no time for God to have been created.
- Others think the idea of God is so ridiculous that they make a movie about it!

In this book I hope you will find out why that is not necessarily true.

Boomers can pose some really hard questions and it is really hard to pull the wool over most Baby Boomer's eyes - it seems like we have seen it all!

- We questioned authority
- We trusted no one over 30!
- We were and still are ... unique
- Sometimes this was good
- Sometimes this didn't work out too well!
- Times were changing and it was like no other time since and ...

We got to see it all in color!

I struggled for several decades of my adult life trying to reconcile what I was taught about God and religion in my youth and what I had learned about science and life. I have come to believe two things:

- Science and God are totally compatible!
- A Life of Hope is a good way to go!

"In sixty-nine I was twenty-one and I called the road my own
I don't know when that road turned on to the road I'm on" — Jackson Browne 1973

Our generation was caught in the middle -between our Depression/World War II-era parents and teachers who had very traditional values and a new way of thinking. Historians can trace the beginnings of the Cultural Revolution of the late 1960's to a new awareness by the younger generation of the times. They called us "Baby Boomers" and there were a lot of us.

There were changes everywhere:

- Women's Liberation
- Black Power
- The Civil Rights movement
- Gay rights
- The Sexual Revolution
- Recreational Drugs
- Civil Disobedience

- Anti-War protests climaxing on the campus of Kent State

Everything seemed to change and to be in conflict; the music of the day reflected our thoughts - it was Dylan versus The Green Beret; Elvis gave way to the Beatles and the Stones.

For many, religion had become irrelevant and out of touch with the realities of this New Age – some called it the Age of Aquarius.

> *"No more falsehoods or derisions*
> *Golden living dreams of visions*
> *Mystic crystal revelation*
> *And the mind's true liberation*
> *Aquarius! Aquarius!"*

Religion did not escape the examination of our generation.

- We questioned what we had been told by the older generation.
  - If people in the past had been so wrong about human rights and war ...

What else had they told us that needed scrutiny?

We couldn't just accept things without questioning!

We felt obligated to find the truth!

Here's the straight scoop.

- No one **knows** whether there is a God or not.
    - It cannot be scientifically proven, one way or the other.
        - Some believe there is a God.
        - Others believe there is not a God.
        - Many have no opinion.

- Those that BELIEVE in God strive to believe in Him 100%.
- They have Faith that God exists.
    - No one is perfect - that is why we need God.
        - Believers often fall short of 100% Faith.
        - How do we know that?

- Because with 100% Faith we should be able to move mountains!

Who has moved a mountain lately?

What we are saying is …
Don't think that you must have 100% perfect
Faith before you can strive for a relationship with
Him.

You Should Know:

Moving mountains is not a requirement.

- God wants you to give Him the benefit of the doubt!
- God is perhaps different than you think!

Maybe some of the Boomers reading this still think that God is:

- "Old Man in White Robes"

- "Myth"
- "The way ignorant people explain what they don't know"

*IF YOU CAN BELIEVE THAT GOD **COULD** EXIST - THEN YOU ARE PART WAY THERE!*

- CAN YOU KEEP AN OPEN MIND?
- MAYBE EVEN MUSTER A LITTLE BIT OF FAITH?

Why you should believe in God can be argued through logic. I find it remarkable that it took so many years and such a great mind to put this simple idea into words.

Blasé Pasqual (1623 – 1662) was a French physicist, inventor, writer, mathematician and Christian philosopher. As a child prodigy, who worked on mechanical calculators and wrote a significant treatise on geometry at age 16. Such was his contribution to math and science that there is a modern computer language, Pascal, named after him.

The famous Pasqual's Wager goes as follows:

The wager uses the following logic *(excerpts from Pensées, part III, §233):*

- God is, or God is not.

- A Game is being played... heads or tails will turn up.

- You must wager.
- Let us weigh the gain and the loss in wagering that God is.
    - If you gain, you gain all;
    - if you lose, you lose nothing.

Wager, then, without hesitation that He is.

But some cannot believe.

They should then ...

"Endeavor ... to convince themselves."

Would Pasqual think you are a Fool?

Belief in God is wise —and therefore NOT to believe in God is unwise or foolish. What harm will come to you if you gamble on its truth and it proves false? Here is what your life would be like:

- **You live a life with belief in God.**
- **You try to be a good person.**
- **You try to do what you think is right in the eyes of God.**
- **You live and die with Hope!**

WHAT IF THEN, YOUR BODY LIES COLDLY IN THE GRAVE AND DECAYS INTO DUST ...

IN OTHER WORDS, NOTHING HAPPENS?

Will you have regrets and think ...

> *"Wow, I must have been wrong about that God thing! – I wish I could go back and have an affair with Marilyn Monroe!"*

Will you be worse off because Hope and Faith were in your life?

Of course not!

Your WORST FEAR for your existence as a Believer is the same as the BEST HOPE of the atheist!

In other words, your choice of God is a winning choice - you have nothing to lose!

So what will you choose - God or no God?

Pasqual's Wager **requires** you to make a choice and the God of Abraham requires that you choose just One.

We all lack PROOF of God or not, but we must make a choice anyway -

Heads or Tails?

... but first consider what it takes to believe in God.

Faith is defined as a belief that is not based on proof.

*The definition of Faith is a belief in God that is not based on proof; faith (without the capital F) is any belief (however ill-founded it may be). For example:

"I have faith that the Falcons will win the Super Bowl."

The Bible says a tiny amount of Faith is all it takes. Just like a seed, Faith can grow into something big - a mighty tree. You just have to nurture it.

"Tiny" is the word used to describe just how little Faith we have to have in order to begin a relationship with God. (In later pages, BBG will talk about what a "relationship with

God" really means, but for now just know that this is a good thing.)

What if you are not 100% Convinced about this God thing?

Have you noticed that hardly anyone these days is declaring themselves to be 100% perfect?

Frankly, it would be hard to find any Believer who has not had doubts, reservations or moments of disobedience to what God wants for us.

The list of people who have publicly admitted to have moments of doubt in God is a long one. It includes me and many of the people around me; it even includes people like Billy Graham, who professed to have moments in his life where he questioned God.

"O God! There are many things in this book I do not understand. There are many problems with it for which I have no solution. There are many seeming contradictions. There are some areas in it that do not seem to correlate with modern science. I can't answer some of the philosophical and psychological questions … others are raising."

Here is the point:
Just give God a little bit of room to work in your spirit - let Him in!

Here is my own personal experience:

"There was a time in my life when I thought I had nothing left to lose - so why not believe? Nothing else seemed to be working out all that great! You hear it from people about how Faith in God changed their lives - I also experienced a change.

The change was for the better, God began to work in my life - or was it a crazy, improbable set of coincidences?

I believe it was God- impossible as it might sound to some; God has ways of letting you know it is Him at work, kind of a calling card from the Spirit.

I will, at some point, share some stories about how God let himself be known to me in a more personal way. Once I became a believer I could begin to sense God even more than ever before. But stories of what happened to me, won't convince you of anything - you need to experience it for yourself to really understand. Thanks to God from Steve!

You can do this!

- He is willing to accept you with just a little, tiny speck of Belief on your part.
- He made you ...you didn't make Him.
  - He is the Boss
  - He wants a relationship with you.

- He gave us the freedom to make our own choice.
  - He is not going to force you to believe in Him
    - although sometimes …He may be forceful
    in trying to get your attention.

You must take the first step!

Just say to Him,

"Yes, I want to believe in You! Show me the way!"

Next find out how you can believe in God.

What, Where, When, How, Who and Why

"There is something even bigger than our Universe - it is called "Existence". Existence is not only the 93 billion light year span that is today's limit of our own observable Universe, but what is beyond. It would include all Universes - Existence is a synonym for everything."

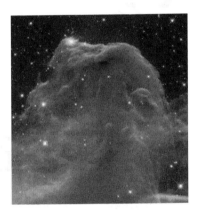

An examination of our Universe and all of Existence seems like it should begin with answering these basic questions.

Science can address:

- **What** is our Universe? What were the building materials?
- **Where** is our Universe? Are we alone? Are there other Universes?
- **When** did our Universe begin?
- **How** did our Universe begin? What forces were at work?

Spirituality can address:

- **Who** - is there a "Who" in our Universe?
- **Why** is there a Universe?

We should never look to Science to answer questions of Spirituality - *it cannot be "observed or measured" as required by the scientific method.*

One professor claims in the name of science that "intelligence cannot exist without a body or a brain". *

- That is a bold statement - since science doesn't even know how our own human intelligence works - how can science, make such a claim?
- There are many things beyond the limits of human intelligence to understand, but in an infinite and eternal Existence –even Science see few constraints.
  - In other words, anything that *CAN* happen *WILL* happen.
- There could most surely be a form of Intelligence that has never before been observed by scientific instrument.
  - Why does this seem impossible to some?

- Did the Universe just happen- randomly and spontaneously?

We must turn elsewhere for an answer.

We want to closely examine these questions:

- Who is this Being?
- Who is in charge?

If there is not a "Who" - then there is not a "Why." This would mean that there is no meaning or reason for Existence –

... *what a lonely thought!*

Several hundred never before seen galaxies are visible in this "deepest-ever" view of the universe, called the Hubble Deep Field (HDF), made with NASA's Hubble Space Telescope.

A Higher Power

First of all to ask, "Who", is to ask- was it a HUMAN PERSON involved in the creation of our universe?

Clearly, this was not the work of any human.

To really answer the question - "Who" created our Universe - we have to look to a concept called Spirituality.

Spirituality

Spirituality is the idea that a Higher Power was, and is, in control of Existence. In other words, everything is being intelligently controlled by "Something" rather than just being a set of spontaneous and random events.

- Spirituality says intelligence does not require a brain as we know it.
    - An "Intelligent Being" exists that is not made of human flesh.
    - Science does say that matter and energy are the same thing.
        - So why would intelligence require matter to be able to have thought?
- We believe there is a Spirit that we think of as - "Who".
    - Supreme thought and intelligence comes from this Spirit of Existence.

The idea of a Higher Power has been viewed differently by mankind throughout history and around the world – but we commonly agree that this Power is bigger than us in all ways.

- We think of the Higher Power as a "Him" and in special roles such as Creator, Father and Judge.
- We are in fear of Him and at the same time we want to learn more.
- Because we share a spirit that is similar to His - we think of Him as our Spiritual Father.

We are not alone in this belief - Native Americans believed in a Great Spirit.

Others may see Karma as a Power providing some order to the world. Rewarding the good and punishing the bad.

Is our God the Higher Power?

Which God is the Higher Power?

There are those who believe in gods - but I would submit to you that there is one God.

- **If there is a God ...**
- **Don't you think He would have tried to communicate with us?**
  - God communicates with many through the magnificence of His work.
    - The splendor of the universe, earth and life!
  - We were born with the ability to know right from wrong.
  - In writing!
    - Why would He have gone to all the trouble?
      - Without telling us who He is
      - Or what He wants with us!
    - We believe that the Bible:
      - That is Holy to three major Faiths
      - Is the word of God.

God described in the Bible:

- **God is:**
    - The God of Abraham
    - Unlimited Spirit, Force and Energy
    - Pervasive throughout Existence.
    - Too vast for human comprehension.
        - He would span the 93 billion light years of our observable universe.

God is not:

- A person.
- A man or a woman.
- *Bound* by the physical limitations of human beings
- *Bound* by any limits of space, nature or time.

Not an "Old Man in White Robes in the Clouds"

To believe that there is God - requires recognition of a Force in Existence that is:

- Infinite and Eternal
- Intelligent
- In control of the physical and Spiritual.
- Good and Just

He would have caused to be created

- Our Universe - Existence - Everything
- Earth
- Life

A starting point on the path to Believing in God - requires that you accept God by Faith.

You must make a conscious decision to Believe.

Believers think that:

- God provides a way for people to live a happy, joyful and hopeful life.
- Eventually, we escape the bounds of a physical life for a spiritual existence.
  - Whether our Spiritual Existence is good or bad - is up to us.

Who is Our God?

The belief that there is a "Who" in the Universe requires that you believe in a Higher Power.   We can come to know Him in minds, hearts and souls.

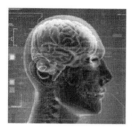 **In Our Minds**

We have rational, conscious thoughts and ideas about our God.

- The concept of God, what He is like and what He expects of us is written in the Bible.

This is the same God sacred to Christianity, Judaism and Islam and therefore known throughout the world.

- Ideas and thoughts about God and what He expects from us can come from reading the Bible.
  - This helps form our mind's eye view of God, but remember that God is so vast, that we humans are only able to sense small parts of God.
    - He is infinite
    - He is a Force, a Spirit, a Supreme Intelligence and Energy
    - Some think we may never visually see God with our eyes, not even in Heaven.
    - We may see different things at times - but God never changes - it is our perception of Him that is changing all the time- as we grow in the Spirit and see new sides of Him

- *It is true, that you have to have Belief in our God to accept what is written by Him through others.*
  - *We understand that it won't be proof of His existence but if you Believe*
    - *The Bible has a lot in store for you.*

God in Us

Human beings share some important traits when it comes to matters of the Spirit.

We all seem to know:

- **Right and Wrong**

Instinctively within all human beings there is thought to be an ability to determine - right from wrong. Nearly all cultures have recognized that certain basic actions or behaviors were in conflict with the idea of being a righteous person. Murder is universally regarded as bad, for example. Believers would say this is like a compass embedded in our soul for recognizing good and evil.

- **Hope**

Also a part of our human makeup is the awareness of our own mortality.

- We bury our dead and remember them and long to see them again.
- We know that someday we will die.
- The possibility of an afterlife has driven man to seek comfort in religions of all sorts.
- We who Believe have Hope for the future
  - Believe that our God is the one True God of the Universe
    - We reject all others.
  - We believe that this God has a plan for us!

The Who of Our Universe and all Existence

That there is a God - is something that we can't prove to science or to you. This will require you to accept as fact, "The Theory of an Intelligent Being in Existence".

About No and Don't Know!

In Pasqual's Wager you are required to make a choice, in life there is no such rule - you can be undecided.

Before you decide:

- You should probably know that God has already made the decision about you according to what He has written.
    - The answer is - if you do not know God then it is a "NO".
        - In other words, if you just want to let the answer to be "NO" - then you don't need to do anything.
    - "NO" is the default - we are not perfect as is - without reconciliation to God for our imperfect spirits.

Your choice then is either you are with Him or you are against Him. There is no other choice!

- The real question is ... are you ready to say - Yes!
- If not, then when will you be ready to say "Yes"?
- Will you say "Yes" now or on your death bed?

Or will you just go to your grave without ever making Peace with God?

Here is something we hear quite often:

"The Bible is wrong, because I found a verse (or more) that I don't believe, therefore the whole thing is bogus."

Invalidating the whole book because there is something that you don't believe or can't understand is like throwing out the baby with the bathwater.

God used human beings to write what would later become books of the Bible. The books were written for the people of that time, yet they are still amazingly relevant today.

Is there any other book your know of that has withstood the four-thousand year test of time?

READING THE BIBLE

The Bible is a very rich and complex document:

- It is not easy to read.
- It has layer upon layer of meaning in its pages.
- People who try to pick up the Bible to read it - often get stuck somewhere in Leviticus!

Try This

Some think a better way to read the Bible is to read it in this order:

- Genesis and Exodus for the history and stories of man's earliest encounters with God.
- The Gospels of Luke and John
- Acts and Romans
- Then read other parts as you are led.

The Bible is to be interpreted by the reader (Christians believe with the help of God's Spirit). Parts of the Bible can be taken:

- Literally only
- Literally and Spiritually
- Spiritually only

The challenge is to know what interpretation to take and when! I won't lie to you ... it is sometimes very hard to understand what God is saying to us. But with the God's help - you can come to understand.

Many of the misconceptions, let's call them stumbling blocks, that we deal with today comes from a misguided interpretation of God's meaning in the Bible. (more on this later!)

There are many versions of the Bible - unless you also want to deal with 17th Century English - you might want to try:

- NIV
- The Living Bible
- The Message
- The Story

I have read the Bible in its entirety once as a skeptic, and subsequently as a believer. Here is what I have found:

- I am not a Biblical expert but I do know that each time I read the Bible I uncovered new thoughts, ideas and insights into the mind of God.
- The key is to read that Bible as someone who is searching for the Truth and not as one who is searching for faults.
- We know that the authors of the Bible were imperfect humans...
- The end result is that there is a Message that Christians can agree upon:

"The Bible delivers the Truths that God intends for us to hear."

Congratulations you have decided to Believe in God!

Haven't you?

(If not maybe you can read some more and ask God to help you with your disbelief!)

Through this belief you are a member of the ranks of "People of the Book".

- This includes:
    - Christian
    - Jewish
    - Muslim

    ... About 54% of the world population.

But is this where we must part?

**I am only able to discuss how Christians can
begin their journey to a Relationship with God.**

*If you are looking for more information about Judaism or
Islam - I can't help you.*

*You will have to go elsewhere, armed with your Belief in
God.*

Peace!

**If you want to learn more about Christianity read
on!**

Did Jesus Christ Exist?

We would answer by saying yes, we believe Jesus did exist and that He was of God.

Those who believe in Jesus Christ say that:

- He was the Messiah spoken of in the Old Testament - parts of which are sacred to all the People of the Book.
- He is the central subject in every part of the New Testament.
- He was sent by God to provide a way to reconcile less than perfect humans with a Perfect God.
- You will hear about Jesus spoken of as the Son of God -

- Some say that He was God himself who came to earth as a Man full of God's Spirit.
- He told us and showed us how to live a better life by being closer to God.
- His words are recorded in the New Testament which gives an account of this man and his deeds.

Flavius Josephus, the secular historian of the period said:

Antiquities 18.3.3. "Now there was about this time Jesus, a wise man, if it be lawful to call him a man, for he was a doer of wonderful works, a teacher of such men as receive the truth with pleasure. He drew over to him both many of the Jews, and many of the Gentiles. He was the Christ; and when Pilate, at the suggestion of the principal men amongst us, had condemned him to the cross, those that loved him at the first did not forsake him, for he appeared to them alive again the third day, as the divine prophets had foretold these and ten thousand other wonderful things concerning him; and the tribe of Christians, so named from him, are not extinct to this day."

Where are the Disputes?

One of the strongest arguments that Jesus truly existed and actually performed the miracles that are written in the

New Testament is the lack of response from the Jewish leaders of the time.

Wouldn't they have disputed claims of miracles more vehemently?

The Pharisees hated Jesus, so why did they not deny that he ever lived and that He had been resurrected?

The fact is that the secular world, historians and even skeptics agree that a man named Jesus Christ lived and then died in his early adulthood in about the year 33.

- Most agree that the impact that this man had was unlike that of anyone who has ever lived
  - He is the most important and influential "person" being who ever lived

- Whether you believe Jesus was divine or not!
- Undisputed Biblical accounts tell us that Jesus showed us that He was from God - by performing miracles.
- He showed us how to live life.
- He was free of sin.
- He was sacrificed to pay "the fine" for all sins.
  - Sins that have been, were and will be committed
    - But not by Him but by mankind.
    - Belief in the Sacrifice of Jesus Christ one of the main Principles of Christian Salvation.

How you can have Jesus Christ in a relationship with God is next.

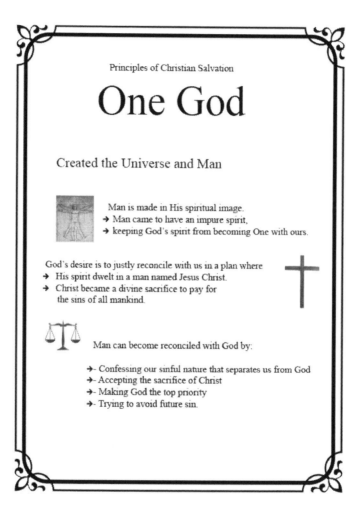

Principles of Christian Salvation

One God

Created the Universe and Man

Man is made in His spiritual image.
➜ Man came to have an impure spirit,
➜ keeping God's spirit from becoming One with ours.

God's desire is to justly reconcile with us in a plan where
➜ His spirit dwelt in a man named Jesus Christ.
➜ Christ became a divine sacrifice to pay for
the sins of all mankind.

Man can become reconciled with God by:

➜- Confessing our sinful nature that separates us from God
➜- Accepting the sacrifice of Christ
➜- Making God the top priority
➜- Trying to avoid future sin.

Here it is one more time ....

    One God

- *Created the Universe and Man*
  - *Man is made in His spiritual image.*
    - *Man came to have an impure spirit,*
    - *keeping God's spirit from becoming One with ours.*
- *God's desire is to justly reconcile with us in a plan where*
  - *His spirit dwelt in a man named Jesus Christ.*
  - *Christ became a divine sacrifice to pay for the sins of all mankind.*
- *Man can become reconciled with God by:*
  - *Confessing our sinful nature that separates us from God*
  - *Accepting the sacrifice of Christ*
  - *Making God the top priority*
  - *Trying to avoid future sin.*

Anything else is unimportant to a Christian - all you have to do to accept this gift is to pray a prayer of salvation and to mean it from the bottom of your heart. The following page has Prayers of Salvation from several different Christian Denominations. If you are ready - your journey can begin!

Here are some prayers to begin a relationship with God.

No lip service please!
This is something that you must take to Heart!

> *Lord Jesus, I know that I am a sinner and I do not deserve eternal life. But, I believe You died and rose from the grave to make me a new creation and to prepare me to dwell in your presence forever. Jesus, come into my life, take control of my life, forgive my sins and save me. I am now placing my trust in You alone for my salvation and I accept your free gift of eternal life."*
>
> *Dear God, I realize that I am a sinner who needs forgiveness. I believe that Jesus Christ died for my sin. I want to turn from sin. Jesus, come into my heart and be Lord of my life. Amen.*

Heavenly Father, I've sinned against you. I want forgiveness for my sins. I believe that Jesus died on a cross and rose again. Father, I give you my life to do with as you wish. I want Jesus Christ to come into my life and into my heart. This I ask in Jesus Name. Amen.

Dear Lord Jesus, I know that I am a sinner and need your forgiveness. I believe that only you can forgive sins. I ask you to come into my heart, forgive my sins, and be the ruler of my life. Thank you for saving me from my sins. Thank you for the love that you show me every day. I now know that eternal life is a gift given from you. I pray and ask that you be the Lord of my life, lead me, guide me and direct my path that I may walk each and every day with you Lord. In your wonderful name I pray. Amen.

These are Prayers of Salvation from several different Christian denominations. You can see these are essentially the same and capture the bottom line of what God asks us to do!

So go ahead and pick one or pray your own prayer to God that admits that you are a Sinner and accept His Sacrifice of Jesus Christ. Ask for Him to come into your life, to guide you and promise you will Obey* Him.

* You Boomers may be wondering if you can live up to that "Obey Him" part?

- If you fail to obey God, and everyone does in their humanity, you will be forgiven.
    - The Bible warns this is not a license to Sin!
- You should vow to try your best, with God's help.
    - He will help you with things that have become tiresome, abusive or have become unhealthy priorities in your life.

God's Plan

Finding what God's plan is for you can be a real adventure! Living a life that you think is significant in the eyes of God has great rewards. These rewards may not always be worldly rewards, it doesn't work that way! The rewards come in a joy of the spirit when you know you are pleasing God and being obedient to what He wants for you.

"Teacher, I will follow you wherever you go."

I remember turning over a calendar page at a Christian mission house in Bangkok a few years ago and getting chills down my back when I read those words. I was really hoping He didn't want me to go to Myanmar or Iran or North Korea! Apparently He didn't.

Whatever calling you or I have depends upon God. We all have a different role to play.

- In the beginning maybe it is just to learn more about God and His Word.
- It is up to us to try to understand what it is that God ultimately would have us do.
- Follow what is in your heart and soul through prayer.

Beware of these things:

- **A "Prosperity" Gospel.**
  - God through Christ does not guarantee you wealth here on Earth; only in Heaven.

  - Nor does He guarantee you what is even more valuable:
    - Health
    - Time.

- **"Religion"**
  - "Religion" is an institution created by man designed to worship and study what is Holy.

- When guided by man alone - it usually doesn't work out so well!
- False "Religion" has turned so many away from the Truth in the past.

- This is not what God intends

- **"Religion" *with* the guidance of God is good!**

- **Apathy**
  - As a Boomer, you know how this works by now.
  - If you are serious about anything you have to go for it!

God's Plan for the World

- The good news is that there is a Plan!
- The bad news is that:
- It is hard to fully understand what He has in store for the World.
  - He gives us glimpses of His Plan in the Bible.
  - It is subject to a lot of interpretation and debate.
  - Some Christians like to speculate on when the "End of the World"* will come.
    - The Bible says "about that day or hour no one knows".

*The End of the World:

- Will come someday when the Sun flames out or sooner.
- Your End of the World can come at any time.

- *Do not text and drive!*
- Understanding what, when and how is not a fundamental part of being a Christian.

We can just say …

"I'm cool with whatever … God is in Charge!"

WHAT DO YOU HAVE TO LOSE?

At this stage, let's assume that you have a little tiny bit of Faith and have said to yourself,

"Why not? Let's go for it!"

Now is the time to nurture this little seed!

From one Boomer to another:

FINDING PEACE!

A lot of Boomers have told me that they are down on "Religion". Just remember that there is a vast difference between some things that call themselves "Religion" and what is *Holy*.

Do not confuse the two!

- Institutions of religion are always imperfect because they are run by humans.
- Humans are flawed and mess up even when they are trying to do their best.
- There are certainly charlatans!
    - There always has been and there always will be.

THIS DOES NOT NECESSARILY MAKE THINGS LIKE CHURCHES AND THE PEOPLE THAT ATTEND THEM BAD!

God and Jesus Christ are what is important.

NOT:

- Denominations
- Doctrine
- Dogma

Discover what is Holy!

- **Bible**

  Seek to understand what God is trying to tell you as you read.

- **Prayer**

  Prayer doesn't always require you to be on your knees. Try just having a conversation with God while you are driving to work. (It is safer than texting!)

- **Church**

  Look for a Church that can teach you more about what is in the Bible.

  Keep trying - go to Churches until you find one that is like home to you.

- **Sharing**

We do have one this one job to do and it is called
the Great Commission - it was Jesus' last words to
all Christians.

"Go and make disciples of all nations!"

"Forever Young"

"May God bless and keep you always
May your wishes all come true
May you always do for others
And let others do for you
May you build a ladder to the stars
And climb on every rung

May you stay forever young
Forever young, forever young
May you stay forever young.

May you grow up to be righteous
May you grow up to be true
May you always know the truth
And see the lights surrounding you
May you always be courageous
Stand upright and be strong

May your hands always be busy
May your feet always be swift
May you have a strong foundation
When the winds of changes shift
May your heart always be joyful
And may your song always be sung

May you stay forever young
Forever young"

"Forever Young"
By Bob Dylan
California 1973

Peace!

Frequently Asked Questions

Here are some good questions. We will try to answer them in the pages that follow.

"How can you believe in a God? That is so ridiculous!"

"Is God Dead?"

"No one can prove that God exists"

"Isn't religion just a way that the ignorant explain away what they don't understand?"

"Hey man, I'm having trouble believing all that!"

"The Bible is wrong, because I found a verse (or more) that I don't believe, therefore the whole thing is bogus."

"The stories of Adam and Eve in a Garden of Eden with a snake, Noah and so on, are not believable to me."

"Fundamentalists are crazy!"

"Christians are judgmental and hypocritical – they think they are better than everyone else."

"Did you know that Christianity and the Church have perpetrated evil in the past and are corrupt?"

"Does God Pull Our Strings?"

"Heaven would be boring! Sitting around in the clouds, playing a harp"

"Why does God Allow bad things to happen?"

> "How can you believe in a God? That is so ridiculous!"

"I can say, coming at it as a scientist, that if you want to feel the majesty of the Universe, you can do it ... without reference to God. "

Science is a philosophy of discovery. Intelligent design is a philosophy of ignorance.

"Someday scientists might unlock all the secrets of the universe, says Dr. Tyson. Then he quickly adds, "Of course, I don't see it on the horizon."

"The more I learn about the universe, the less convinced I am that there's any sort of benevolent force that has anything to do with it, at all."

- Dr. Neil deGrasse Tyson

Dr. Tyson estimates that science understands approximately 6% of what there is to know about the Universe. This means that, up to now, we have just barely scratched the surface of the scientific mysteries of the Cosmos.

Science can describe some things that happened when our Physical Universe was created - like the Big Bang, Evolution and so on.

That is how God would work -using the known and unknown forces of nature to create the Universe and Mankind.

Science cannot address the areas of a Spiritual nature, because it cannot be measured or observed.

- In other words, everyone is entitled to their own opinion and theories, but they will remain scientifically unproven.
- Science is basking in its own glory while remaining ignorant of the workings of 94% of what is around us.
- Scientists are entitled to their own personal opinion about God, but not to declare that opinion as fact.
- According to Science the Universe produced our intelligence by accident.

- Then in an infinite Universe(s) other intelligence must have also been created.
  - Some of this intelligence could be different than we currently understand it
  - Why could not the ultimate of intelligence in the Universe ... be God?

You and I will never answer many of these questions! It is Faith in the unknown that we all must ultimately rely upon:

- Either Faith that the final M-Theory formula will prove something (but we are not sure what!).

or

- Faith that an Intelligent Being somehow brings order to all of Creation.

Scientists should never stop trying to uncover how the Universe was formed and how it functions - this is all very fascinating stuff!

We should not fear anything that science has to say about the what, when, where and how of the Universe and of Life - this is simply a way to explain the Workings of God.

Did you know that no one has proven there is not a God? Not even Dr. Stephen Hawking!

"The emergence of the complex structures capable of supporting intelligent observers seems to be very fragile. The laws of nature form a system that is extremely fine-tuned, and very little in physical law can be altered without destroying the possibility of the development of life as we know it. Were it not for a series of startling coincidences in the precise details of physical law, it seems, humans and similar life-forms would never have come into being." - Hawking, Stephen; Mlodinow, Leonard (2010-09-07). The Grand Design (Kindle Locations 1628-1631). Random House, Inc., Kindle Edition.

"Our universe and its laws appear to have a design that both is tailor-made to support us and, if we are to exist, leaves little room for alteration. That is not easily explained, and raises the natural question of why it is that way." - Hawking, Stephen; Mlodinow, Leonard (2010-09-07). The Grand Design (Kindle Locations 1647-1649). Random House, Inc., Kindle Edition.

To explain: The "starting coincidence" of life on earth, Dr. Hawking uses the MULTIVERSE THEORY.

"...our universe seems to be one of many, each with different laws. That multiverse idea is not a notion invented to account for the miracle of fine-tuning. It is a consequence of the no-boundary condition as well as many other theories of modern cosmology. But if it is true, then the strong anthropic principle can be considered effectively equivalent to the weak one, putting the fine-tunings of physical law on the same footing as the environmental factors, for it means that our cosmic habitat—now the entire observable universe—is only one of many, just as our solar system is one of many. That means that in the same way that the environmental coincidences of our solar system

were rendered unremarkable by the realization that billions of such systems exist, the fine-tunings in the laws of nature can be explained by the existence of multiple universes." - Hawking, Stephen; Mlodinow, Leonard (2010-09-07). The Grand Design (Kindle Locations 1675-1681). Random House, Inc., Kindle Edition.

In other words, the Theory of the Multiverse says there are an:

Infinite Number of Universes!

In this view, there would be an infinite number of Universes, Galaxies, Stars and Planets. This means an infinite number of planets just like earth. On these infinite earths there are an infinite number of people exactly like you – other groups would be *almost* like you.

This is similar to the idea that an infinite number of monkeys with typewriters could eventually write all of Shakespeare's works.

An unanswered question with this Multiverse Theory is:

Could God happen too?

The answer seems to be that –

**He could not help but exist ...
in a Cosmos where anything is possible!**

"The Idea of a God is Preposterous!"

A God of the Universe would have intelligence through some mechanism that we can't even begin to understand. Then again, we can't even figure out how our own brain works!

Science

Science can describe some things that happened when our Physical Universe was created

- Big Bang or Evolution

    o That's the way a God would work -

- Using the known and unknown forces of nature to create the Universe and Mankind.

- Describe the Physical Universe

  - The What, Where, When and How

Science cannot address the Who and Why:

(even though Dr. Stephen Hawking is trying)

- *Because these things can't be observed or measured as required by the Scientific Method.*

Another self-described scientist/philosopher, Quentin P. Smith, Professor of Philosophy at Western Michigan University claims that God is inconsistent with Science and that "that there is no such thing as a mind without a brain or body".

From Closertotruth.com: Are Science & Religion at War?

Really?

- What about Artificial Intelligence, professor? Does this not refute your argument?

    o It does not require a body or a brain.

    o Artificial Intelligence does not require carbon-based matter like flesh or grey brain cells.

    o If mankind can create "Watson" or "Siri" in such a short time - what could happen in infinity and eternity?

    o Science does not know whether there are other types of intelligence or not.

        ▪ *We are certainly not saying that God is a computer, let me be clear on that!*

    o But, we don't even understand our own intelligence and how it works.

    o The preposterous part is to rule out that possibility because it is not like anything we have yet observed.

- We are discovering new things all the time!

Science says:

- Energy and matter are the same thing.
  - Just in different states (like ice and water).
  - So, why couldn't a "brain" be made of energy or spirit instead of matter?
  - Believers say:
    - Spirit is a special type of energy
      - Spirit is the Mind of God

The thing is:

Are you willing to bet everything on Science ...

when they say that a Supreme Intelligence could not have happened just because it doesn't have a brain like us?

The Futility of Science

When it comes to questions of the Spirit – the Who and Why of the Universe – science cannot help!

Baby Boomers may remember the 1966 science fiction movie "Fantastic Voyage" which main attraction was Raquel Welch.

In this movie, scientists in a miniature spaceship, were injected into a human bloodstream and encountered a multitude of problems. During their voyage they saw all kinds of physical structures; blood vessels, heart, nerves, the brain and so on.

The question is:

Would those scientists have the ability to read the mind of the individual that they were a part of, just because they could observe his liver or his brain?

Of course not!

We do not have that ability to read people's minds!

- Science has no instruments to measure this.

- They can see our brain waves - but not our thoughts.

Then what makes us think we can know the Thoughts and the Mind of God by simply observing His Universe with our scientific instruments?

"Aren't Fundamentalists kind of crazy?"

"Fundamentalists' are crazy - they say the Universe was created 6,000 years ago and that the scientists have tricked us about the age of the earth with things like the dinosaurs and cavemen. "

Modern believers can believe that scientific facts of the big bang, evolution and other creation events may certainly be true.

This does not have any bearing on whether there is a God or not. An Intelligent Being would have controlled the Big Bang and the Evolution of man. Science can tell us:

- **What** He did it with
- **Where** He did it
- **When** He did it
- **How** He did it

Christianity should be concerned with Who did it and Why –
not What, Where, When or How!

Does the Bible have to be interpreted literally?

- Some insist that every verse in the Bible has to be interpreted literally.
  - Much of the New Testament refers to the **Spiritual and not the physical.**
    - **Why could not** some of the **Old** Testament stories also be Spiritual and not physical or literal?
    - Why ask people who are interested in God to accept a literal view of creation?
  - Literal interpretation of certain verses of the Old Testament in particular, has led to some of the most shocking and harmful behaviors on the part of Christians. There is a modern day preacher who is calling for the stoning of homosexuals, for example, arguing that the laws in the book of Leviticus be followed to the letter!

What is Truth?

- The Bible contains plenty of Truth - and the best part is the Spiritual part!
- When we insist that everything in the Bible should be interpreted literally.
    - We miss the point!
        - Especially around the year 33 AD - to those who were expecting a real earthly king
            - To lead an army to physically rescue them from the Romans
    - We drive new non-believers away when we ask them to accept the unacceptable

Christ said "you are to be born again!"... Who wants try that literally?

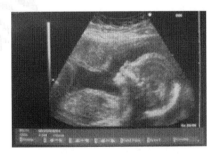

There is an argument for the literal translation of every verse of the Bible that goes something like this:

"You can't take away from the Word of God and you can't add to it!"

The Bible, in my opinion, is not just "black and white". There are more than 50 shades of grey!

There is an underlying Theme that goes something like this:

- God loves you!
- He wants you to love Him!
- He wants you to love others!
- He wants you to tell others about Him!

It is possible to pick verses that seem to contradict this message.

What should we do?

- Look for other verses or at the context of the passage to see if that is really what God intends to say. Or is there some other way to look at it?

- When in doubt, I go to the passages printed in RED – what did Christ Himself say or not say about the topic? The words of Christ are trumps!
- Some passages refer to old laws that a literalist wants to ignore:
  - Shall we stone adulterers?
  - Shall we burn prostitutes?
  - Shall we behead magicians or drunkards?
  - The list goes on and on!
- Pray about it!
  - What does God want you to understand?
- Recognize what is intended to be Spiritual and not literal
  - Much of the New Testament is Spiritual!
    - Many did not comprehend this including:
      - The Disciples
      - The Jewish priests
    - The Jewish people, in their literal view of the Bible, were looking for a PHYSICAL king to free them from the Romans!
      - What happened was a Spiritual King to free us all - Spiritually!
      - Many missed the whole point!

- You cannot PHYSICALLY:
  - Pass a camel through the eye of a needle
  - Be born again
  - Drink the blood of Christ
  - Christ was not actually bread or water
  - And so on

- Then why do many insist that the OLD TESTAMENT be literal? The New Testament or New Covenant of Jesus became a stumbling block for the Jewish people because of literal interpretation of God's word.
- Why do Christians make the same mistake and turn the Old Testament and Old Covenant into a stumbling block for new believers by insisting upon a literal interpretation? Didn't we learn our lesson?

- We are ignoring many of the laws that are not convenient (or intended) for today.
- **This is a MAJOR stumbling block for many Boomer non-believers!**
- **People, especially young people – millennials are leaving Christianity in droves largely due to this issue.**
- Attacks on Christianity often begin with scoffers pointing out what they call absurd beliefs.
  - Certain stories of the Bible were not intended to be physical or literal – in my opinion.
  - Let's don't make the literal interpretation of selected passages be a roadblock to learning about God and Christ!

All you need is Love!

The Moral of the Story is that God loves us and found a way for us to be reconciled to Him, through the sacrifice of Jesus.

- *Christ told a young man that the Greatest Commandments are:*
  - *Love God*
  - *Love one another as yourself*

"On these two commandments hang all the law and the prophets."

Who are we to argue?

We need to Love God and do what God leads us to do!

- This means we must "listen with our hearts" to God...
- He will let us know what He wants and what He doesn't want!

Christianity is not about a bunch of "DOs" and "DO NOTs"!

(When Christians depart from this we mess up!)

- **Christianity is to be driven by Love and Faith - NOT by Rules!**
  - *You cannot "earn" your way into Heaven*
    - *By doing good.*
    - *Or by not doing bad!*
- *We have one important job – it is our Mission given to us by Christ in his LAST WORDS on Earth:*

  "Go and tell others about Me!"

What is Sin?

If you break a "Rule" - then *some* people will call it a SIN!

- Christians should trust the Holy Spirit to convict the other person of their "SIN"
  - ***This is not a JOB for human beings!***

- Some can take a single Bible passage that condemns some sort of SIN
  - Then use this to condemn the Sinner

  (Not good!)

What is a Sin?

Here are some important points for you to remember about Sin!

- ***To God all Sin is the same and is unacceptable.***

- - *This is different than the laws of man – where murder, rape and pedophilia are much worse and punished more harshly than lying or adultery!*
  - *To God there are not various degrees of "Badness"*
    - *Either you are good or you are bad to God*
  - *Therefore, your sin and mine are just as loathsome to God as anything Charles Manson or ISIS have ever done!*
  - *So who do we think we are when we condemn someone else's Sin?*

- If Loving God and Loving Others should be the most important things in our lives …
  - Then anything that gets in the way of this is a Sin.

  - If something becomes more important to you than God:
    - That is a Sin
    - Ask yourself …

"Is this more important to me than it needs to be?"

These things are on my list of potential SINS!

- Fishing
- Golf
- College Football
- Harley Davidson Road Kings
- Pecan Pie
- And so on

... *it is a very long list!*

What is on your list of things to work on?

In your mind, you may be asking,

"What about _____?"

(Insert a thing you do that may be hurting other people, has become too important in your life, is self-destructive or seems to separate you from God).

It could include:

- Addictions of all sorts
- Abuse of self or others
- And more

Here is an answer:

God can and will help people who believe in Him to overcome barriers or roadblocks to having a relationship with Him.

- He can take away some of the desire to do harmful things!
    - Often this is a process and not an instantaneous transformation, as God works in your life.
    - You will hear about Repenting of your Sins.
        - "Repenting" is a process and not a single act.
    - We all "SIN" every day, because we are human!
        - It is the act of TRYING each day that is the act of Repenting
            - Pleasing God is the key
            - The best part is that God is able to forgive us for our SINS! (When we ultimately fall short!)

All else falls into place when you Love God and Love others!

REMEMBER IT IS ABOUT LOVE!

"Why are Christians so Judgmental and Hypocritical?"

Christians can most certainly be judgmental and hypocritical! I am sorry when I have done this and know that many Christians make this mistake too. This doesn't make us all bad! Annoying perhaps; but bad, no!

When we judge - Christians violate several of Jesus Christ's teachings:

- "He, who is without sin, be the first to throw a stone"
- "Do not judge, or you too will be judged"
- "So why do you see the piece of sawdust in another believer's eye and not notice the wooden beam in your own eye?"

Only God knows what is in our hearts.

- No man, except Jesus, has ever been able see what was in men's souls.
    - Do not try to assess someone else's walk with God !
        - But sometimes humans are not able to resist the temptation to judge others behavior and infer from that behavior, the state of other peoples relationship with God.

This is wrong! We know it and we trust that we can be forgiven for this!

When we judge others and then, inevitably, fall short of expectations ourselves – we are certainly being hypocritical.

We all have faults – instead of finding it, maybe we should just forgive and help each other find God! *(This does not including pointing out other peoples warts and telling them that their baby is ugly.)*

What has Love got to do with this?

Let me take a most extreme example to illustrate what can happen when God's message is distorted and Christians think they have to add a requirement to their form of religion.

"A passage in the Mark 16:18 says, "They shall take up serpents; and if they drink any deadly thing, it shall not hurt them." – and to pastor Jamie Coots of Middleboro, Kentucky and others this is to be taken quite literally.

Coots and his followers believe that God calls upon them to handle venomous serpents and to drink other poisons. Even if they are bitten, they will refuse medical treatment because they believe that they are worthy of God's faith, and that their fate is in God's hands.

According to ABC news' Nightline, after Coots' death in February of 2014:

"...Pastor Coots himself had been bitten nine times, and each time he refused medical attention."

When "Nightline" spoke with him at his church in November, Coots scoffed at the notion that he was taking the Bible too literally.

"To me that's what God taught me to be about," he said.

Imagine if Christianity was about - snakes! (Why did it have to be snakes?)

- What a roadblock that would be to "new recruits"!
- The misguided pastor made a mistake.
  - Taking one Biblical passage in isolation is a very dangerous proposition!
  - Indeed, this group could well be served by paying attention to the part of the Bible where Christ said (paraphrased):
    - Do not tempt God by doing foolish things.
    - Expecting Him to intervene and save your life!

- Avoid stubborn and misguided interpretations of what God wants us to do.
    - I'm pretty sure He does not want us handling poisonous snakes.
    - Yet to some this is what it means to be an obedient Christian.

HERE IS ONE THING THAT I BELIEVE - IT WILL BE ANYTHING BUT BORING!

Look inside ↓

Randy Alcorn author of the book - **Heaven** - portrays Heaven as a real and exciting place!

- The Bible says that we are meant to come back to a New Earth that is a paradise.

- To our God that created the Cosmos, this would be fairly light work!

This is just the tip of the iceberg! Use your imagination to explore how you think it will be!

The Apostle Paul said:

"Eye has not seen, nor ear heard, nor have entered into the heart of man
the things which God has prepared for those who love Him"

"I Don't Believe in Adam and Eve"

As for an Adam and Eve –

Here is a scientific answer:

There was most certainly a line of demarcation between early ape-like hominids and the first humans; the Bible tells a story of this in a manner that has been understood and misunderstood though out spiritual history. Undoubtedly at some point in time homo-sapiens crossed a mental or spiritual line, when they became self-aware and aware of their mortality.

Spiritually

Adam and Eve

When the moment of awareness of God happened:

- Mankind came into being through possession of a soul.
  - We think of God as having breathed spiritual life and a soul into mankind.
  - This would be the first real Man and we could call him Adam.

"What about Noah and Jonah and all the rest?"

- These stories were told and passed from generation to generation for centuries and are meant to be understand by the people of that time.
- In a Spiritual sense I believe that these stories contain Truth.
- You should read for understanding. Ask:
  - Is this meant to be spiritual or literal?
  - If spiritual:
    - Answering how, when, where or what He used to do it is not important.
    - *Who* and *why* is a better focus!
- Whether you want to believe a literal translation of this or other Old Testament Biblical story or not.
  - It is up to you.

- It is not a prerequisite for having a relationship with God through Jesus Christ.
  - So why would Christians want to impose a literal belief on others?
    - We should not miss telling the world about the basic principles of Christianity.

TIME MAGAZINE POSED THIS QUESTION IN APRIL OF 1966.

Asking if God is dead is the same as acknowledging that you think - He was Alive at some point.

If you thought He was once alive – why would you think He is dead now?

- Perhaps you think that He has somehow abandoned you or mankind?
- God is who He is. (Maybe not what you may think or what you want Him to be!)
- The best way to find out if God is dead ... is to ask Him!

"Why Would a Good God allow bad things to happen?"

In life, we experience joy and pain. In our physical life, we are tied to the principles of the world. If we step off a cliff, we will fall.

In our Spiritual Life

God cannot exempt anyone from what will happen in their lives here on Earth.

- We all must die someday.
- Many of us will experience the death of a loved one at some point in our lives.
- There are incredibly evil things that happen to God's people.

What if Christians were the only people who never died?

Wouldn't this be forcing people to be a Christian?

I believe that what happens to us and the world, is ultimately the Will of God, whatever that may be.

- He does not administer or wish Evil upon us.
- He has allowed Evil to exist here on earth for a while.

- He does not want us to be slaves to Him, but to be free to choose.

Christians and God-loving people everywhere are subject to the ways and laws of the Universe.

- Accidents happen, people get sick and people die - this is the way of the world.
- What God wishes for us is an eternal life with Him in Heaven.

- Heaven will make all the trials and sufferings that we had to endure here on Earth ... worthwhile.

However, I believe that God can and does intervene in people's lives when He chooses and when it serves His Will and Plans.

When we are faced with something terrible in our lives is when we sometimes question God.

Why would God allow this to happen?

- We will not know the true answer until it is revealed to us by God Himself.
- How a tragedy can lead to something that is part of God's Good Plan is unfathomable to us - but we must trust in Him.

- Trusting God and having Faith in His Plan is what can help us through difficult times.

What is most important in the Grand Scheme is not how we feel about the quality of our short life on earth, but the quality of the rest of eternity.

Early on in the history of Christianity - Believers were tortured, crucified, stoned, fed to wild beasts, burned and beheaded by Roman emperors. Early martyrs were an example to all who followed as to what it means to sacrifice for your Faith.

Sadly, even today Christians and others are being persecuted for what they believe.

God must be weeping!

HERE IS HOW I EARNED MY BABY BOOMERS BADGE:

Steven L. Testerman

I am an author and curator of content here at Baby Boomers Guide.

Born: Carthage, Missouri – 1948
Currently: Living in the Atlanta suburb of Cumming, Georgia

Education:

Parkview High School
Class of 1966
Springfield, Missouri

Missouri State University
Class of 1971

B.S. Economics
Kappa Alpha Order
Springfield, Missouri

Military:

USMCR – Marine Corps Recruit Depot, San Diego -
August, 1969
2nd Lieutenant - U.S. Army Reserve - 1974

Career:

- Author | Business Owner/ CEO | Entrepreneur
- Financial Services | Technology

Other Stuff:

- Christian
  - Adult Sunday School Teacher
  - Children's Ministry
  - Foreign Missions - Thailand
- Father and Grandfather
- Scout Leader and Eagle Scout
- Student of History and Science

Bullet points don't tell the story though!

I'm just a regular guy - not a preacher or a scientist - with a hope to bring some understanding to Baby Boomers who are still questioning the very existence of God.

I want to present to you some of the most current thinking from a variety of sources including leaders in the scientific, secular and religious communities and share some of my own thoughts too.

This case for God is intended to be:

- Easy-to-follow and Logical
    - Let's face it - we have the attention span of a gnat!
        - Bullet-points help you understand content more quickly.
        - No extensive quoting of scripture
            - Search for references on your own.
- Modern
    - Science and technology have challenged our previous concepts of God.
        - We will explore today's thoughts in the "War between Science and Religion"

- Hawking, Tyson, Maher and others challenge the existence of God.
  - Have they proven it? (Read on to find out the strait scoop.)

My own philosophy is that of a Christian, but I won't promote any certain denomination of the Faith.

I believe that Christians should:

- Squabble less over minutia and ritual.
- Focus more about sharing our Faith with the world.

My own path to Christianity wasn't an easy one - full of Baby Boomer hills and valleys - but I'm still here today after all these years wanting to share what little I have learned these past 50-years or so. Draw your own conclusions.

I will try my best to present a rational case supporting the existence of God.

Draw your own conclusions.

Regardless of what you decide ...

Peace!

I'm including these notes hoping that there is some insight in these for someone who is still searching.

I believe that the religious landscape has not escaped the changes in society over the last 50 years – and I think that by some measures "religion" has become more open and aligned with biblical precepts than ever before.

- That doesn't mean it has no room for development.
- Spiritual growth and change seems to me, to be one of the slowest to change of all of our human endeavors.
    - This is not all bad - it prevents religious thought from swinging with current fashion and fad.
    - But when religious thinking collides with new scientific facts and new theories - as has happened and accelerated over the last half of the 20th century – the result is something like when two power weather fronts collide creating a maelstrom.

- The result is a generation at risk of being lost -and there is a price to pay for being lost.

Spiritually, I'm very much a product of my youth and exposure to religious things during my teenage years. In this I have found I am not alone. Many begin their exposure to spiritual things at a time you might call an age of conscience or of accountability. During this time, even if it never happens again in our lives, nearly everyone, it seems, searches for answers to questions about being, about life and its meaning. Some get the answers they are looking for and others may just decide to "table it" until they can get more information.

As for me, it has been my lifetime quest to try to discover truth and try to reconcile or justify what seems to be inconsistencies; in what is being taught in our schools, what is in the media and what our culture perceives to be the existence and role of God in our lives. Often times the road to justifiable beliefs in a greater power begins with the question of creation and it is here where the first test comes for those seeking answers.

We have a need to be able to justify things that are unobservable, or unproven like certain theories of the Cosmos or of God. It is tough wrapping our brains around big things like infinity, eternity, a light year or a billion dollars!

To me all the Theories of the Universe including the Theory of God - are incredibly complex and are possibly beyond the capacity of any man to understand. There are so many questions to be answered.

Science only understands a small part of what there is to know about the Universe and can only address those things it can measure. Today, many are confused by opinions of prominent scientists; astrophysicists, astronomers and others who garner news headlines with proclamations such as, "There didn't have to be a God" or "God did not have time to exist."

Many people my age have asked me the same exact questions when they find out that I believe in God and am willing to publicly admit and defend not only the existence of God, but also of His Plan for the us through Jesus Christ.

These questions have led me to my ministry through Baby Boomers Guide, trying to reach my peers who have the same questions that I once asked myself.

My Background.

Growing up in Springfield, Missouri, as a teenager in the early 1960, I was immersed in what has been called Midwestern values and was at ground zero of the Bible belt. Springfield has been called the most "churched" city in the US and is the headquarters of the Assemblies of God – one of the largest Pentecostal, evangelical denominations, as well as Christian colleges for the Baptist and AG denominations. There was certainly no lack of opportunity for access to Christian thinking and the environment was as conducive to spiritual morality and practice, I suspect, as any that may have existed anywhere during this time.

My spiritual background developed due to family background, in the Assembly of God church – a church with the distinguishing belief in the modern day spiritual gifts of speaking in tongues and the interpretation of these messages from God. I make no judgments here, and I myself spoke in tongues at the early age of 13 – in what felt like a real religious experience.

I was however aware that this was considered by many, even in the headquarters city of the Assembly of God, to be an unusual, perhaps weird, practice – I remember being with a friend, being driven somewhere by his parents, and passing my Church, he said "That's where the Holy Rollers go to church". I didn't have the nerve to tell him the truth.

The issues that I had with the Church was not speaking in tongues; the problem came, as with many, many people I have spoken to about faith, during my teenage years and in trying to live the life that I was called upon to live by my church. I eventually rebelled.

I rebelled against the rules of this church, which were at that time: No dancing, no movies, no makeup for women and modest clothing. And of course, no drinking, smoking, cussing or as it seemed to a teenager – no fun at all! It turns out that the rules of this church and the "rules" of many churches turn out to not be based on the Bible, but just what some Church leaders thought should and would be proper behavior for its members.

I remember asking my Sunday school teacher, if not going to movies included movies like The Ten Commandments. His reply was that yes, we should not see it or other Biblical movies, which were popular at the time, because "there will inevitably be a scene were scantily dressed women will perform a pagan dance". Furthermore, the church argued that patronizing movies only helped "Hollywood" profit from degrading our moral fiber.

Dancing was another no-no, it seems that church leaders were not comfortable with young teenagers writhing in pleasure that might have a sexual element to it, to a very questionable type of music – Rock and Roll! Therefore, dancing is a sin, or at least what you thought in your mind while you were holding a member of the opposite sex close to your body certainly was!

The worst part of all this, was that it detracts from the core message and to set up a non-biblically based, man-made rule as a barrier to anyone who might otherwise want to learn more.

It seemed like a religion based upon what you SHALL NOT do. Not one based upon the true core foundation of Christianity – or at least the basics were so lost in the message – that it took me many years to understand what is really a very simply premise. They lost me for a while and what is more distressing – I lost myself along the way. But I know now that I was not lost to God.

 The penalty for any transgressions, were made vividly clear each and every Sunday in sermons and tortuous altar calls. These moments called for every head to be bowed and every eye to be closed, while the preacher invoked every persuasion to get sinners out of their seats and on their knees at the altar to beg for forgiveness. I remember thinking that the preacher was talking directly to me when he spoke of lost sinners, as he made me feel the weight of all that had gone on that week to condemn me!

The anxiety was pretty intense at times; I remember being on the verge of panic attacks from the guilt that I felt and for the price that I was told I would have to pay for my sins.

If I had read the part of the Bible that says that nothing can take my salvation from me, I might have felt more secure in my previous salvation. In fact, I would come to understand and believe years later that I had been saved at age 13 and I had done nothing to lose that – that all was well and that I should have been experiencing joy in my faith, instead of fear for my transgressions. I think that many Christians could take more joy in the proclamation in Romans that nothing can take your salvation from you.

The consequences of remaining still, it seemed, was an eternity of everlasting Hell – a lake of fire, torture beyond comprehension, separation from God and all that is good. The only thing to do was to drop down to your knees at the altar each week and amid much shame for the weak lowlife that you are – to plead with God for forgiveness and a renewal of your salvation.

Repentance was the watchword – repenting constantly, while being reminded that Christ said "go and sin no more"! No one ever suggested or reminded us that Paul himself, found repentance impossible to achieve – try as he may. No one ever suggested that you were forgiven in salvation for not only you previous sins, but also for your future sins!

The Assemblies of God were not the only ones to overlook this biblical concept – the idea is one of confession of sin. Yet nowhere in the Bible is there a stipulation or an asterisk to salvation – confession of every sin before your death.

The Last Rites practiced by some Catholic believers seems to suggest that without a confession of your sins before death that you are lost – not Biblical or true in my estimation, that being one with God ensures forgiveness for all sins – past, present and future – it is not a conditional forgiveness based upon never sinning again. Never sinning again is not possible!

Mine was a controlling religion, based upon fear of God. Your salvation was never secure it seemed, and you were only safe when you were on your knees praying for forgiveness – heaven forbid that you should utter a curse word on your way home from Church, in the event that you found a semi-truck in you lane and went to face eternity with that blemish on your record!

The End of the World

The fascination with this topic, that some embrace - is an interesting study. Not only does the poor Christian have to worry about actively maintaining their salvation up to the moment of death or at least be cognizant enough to ask for forgiveness before your final breath – but within a twinkling of an eye, at a time unknowable to anyone, the world is going to end.

This, of course, would make all of your religious works and faith count for naught – because there may be an unforgiven sin still lingering. The answer was to "be ready" or in other words, be in a constant state of repentance or without sin in preparation for instant death and judgment. This created a real anxiety on the part of the believer to do something to keep right with God on a constant basis – just in case.

This may sound a little odd to some who read this, but believe me, in the mind of a 13-year old in the height of the Cuban Missile crisis – the end of the world didn't seem all that unlikely. In fact, I was pretty well convinced that I would not live to see the ripe old age of 21, when I could get married (presumably have sex. Give me a break! I was only 13!), and see what life would be like as an adult.

The prevailing opinion is that this is going to happen very soon – certainly within our lifetime – but most likely within the next year or two. As "all the signs" point to the End – wars, rumors of wars, natural disasters, earthquakes, and more – the time for action was now! Those who are fascinated with this topic attempt to interpret the books of the Bible dealing with this topic such as Revelations and Daniel.

The answer to all this is contained within the very text that they try to decipher – no one knows when the End of the World will come! And surely, we all know that ultimately this will be true – the sun will burn out, or some other event natural or man-made will bring on the end of our species existence.

I happen to believe that God does have a plan for the End of the World. There is nothing that we need to do (unless called upon by God) to help this plan along, neither is there anything we can do to stop it.

Furthermore, you can't, as a Christian be more ready to die because you think life can end at any moment through an End of the World disaster – the fact is that our individual worlds can, and will, end and that being ready means having accepted the basic Principles of Christianity. There is nothing else to do.

As a technique to control Christians and keep them fearful and pious, maybe the "scare" technique works sometimes – as a lead in to discussing Christianity with non-believers usually it is a "non-starter". We might as well don a robe and sandals, and carry a placard declaring "The End is Near". See how many souls you can save with that approach!

As a year or two came and went, as I was waiting for the bombs to fly, it occurred to me that the more likely scenario is that an individual's world could end behind the wheel of their '58 Chevy (without seat belts), or while crossing the street or perhaps while eating a fish sandwich.

The End of the World comes to us all, sooner or later, and I don't truly care if I go alone or with lots of company – the result is the same.

The fact is that, in spite of the constant reminder of our imminent fate, the world did not end but that most of the people who sat in that 1961 congregation have passed on. How much more joyous and less anxious might their lives have been without the burden of impending doom. How many in that congregation, were turned away by the tangential teachings of this church, we will never know.

The good news is that this brand of blind fundamentalism has decreased with time – most of the mainstream evangelical churches have relaxed some of the "DO NOTS" in favor of "Why don't we leave the Judgements to God?" After all ... Judgement is His job and definitely not ours!

One thing, I believe to be true, is that when Christians have the opportunity to communicate their beliefs to believers and non-believers alike, we need to be clear, concise and of one voice.

We need to talk about the basic plan of salvation and not to confuse that message with a bunch of "do not's", creating rules and hurdles that block the message and by being judgmental.

Here is the message:

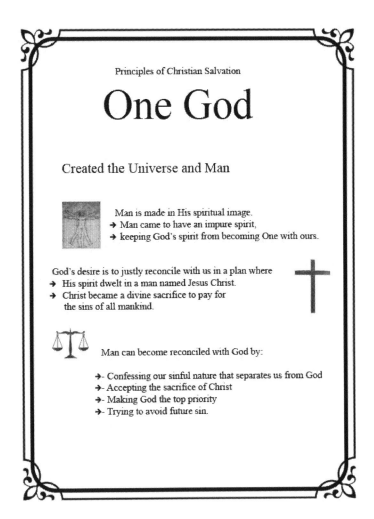

Principles of Christian Salvation

One God

Created the Universe and Man

Man is made in His spiritual image.
→ Man came to have an impure spirit,
→ keeping God's spirit from becoming One with ours.

God's desire is to justly reconcile with us in a plan where
→ His spirit dwelt in a man named Jesus Christ.
→ Christ became a divine sacrifice to pay for
the sins of all mankind.

Man can become reconciled with God by:

→- Confessing our sinful nature that separates us from God
→- Accepting the sacrifice of Christ
→- Making God the top priority
→- Trying to avoid future sin.

My Journey

I wandered away from the experience of my youthful encounter with "Religion". I grew apart from God.

I reached a time in my life when I felt that I had nothing left to lose. I thank God for helping me find my way back from the edge of darkness and showing me how to begin a journey to connect with Him.

What is it in my nature, and that of many others, that makes us ignore God until we need Him the most?

How much easier life would be for us, if we would seek Him out before the crises comes in our lives – and the crises WILL come, sooner or later for us all.

For years, I had struggled with issues arising from my religious experiences as a youth and with reconciling what I believed was necessary to be a Christian with modern thinking.

Science teachers had told me one thing and the Church was telling me that this was not true. The Church was telling me how I had to live and what I could and could not do – and to disobey was eternal damnation. I was told to repent of my sins, and in the words of Christ "Sin no more". I didn't find this easy to do. So as a result, I did nothing – I lived my life as I saw fit, and gave little thought to God – until I was hit between the eyes with the consequences of my neglect.

The problem was not so much as I didn't want to believe and have faith – I was just mislead, confused and suffering from many doubts. I was searching for a rational, believable Supreme Being – one that could ring true in my mind and in my heart – but I could not find Him. I would never admit this to anyone, of course. I decorated the Christmas tree and said grace when I felt I had to – going through some basic motions and paying lip service. I was no Lieutenant Dan – (from Forrest Gump) shaking my fist at God and daring him to strike me down – I preferred to keep a somewhat lower profile than that. I didn't want to make waves.

Then my Life Changed

One day some men came to my apartment – I had gone to a Church and filled out a visitation card. One of them asked me, "If you would die tomorrow would you go to heaven?" I said "yes, of course because I am basically a good person". As soon as the words left my mouth, I knew that this was not how it works – and I did get down on my knees and asked God, though Jesus's sacrifice as payment, to pardon me for my disobedience to Him. And so began by journey.

My mind was set was toward finding out How I can believe and believe more strongly and more completely – not all doubts were instantly gone. I hope you can appreciate the honesty of a self-proclaimed Christian when I tell you that I did not have 100% faith – perhaps I was filled more with Hope than Faith – but I had just enough of both to hold on to! The Bible tells us that we don't really need all that much faith – just like a tiny mustard seed is sufficient – and that it can grow if we nurture it. It also tells us that God can help you in your unbelief and that no human has ever had perfect Faith.

The first issue I had to tackle was the big disconnect between, what I perceived to be sacred as part of my upbringing in the church and what I believed to be scientific facts. This was important for me to understand and to reconcile if my faith were to grow.

Since that time, I have had many conversations, usually initiated by friends, who all begin at the same place – the place that I had been as well.

Some of the questions that they asked are outlined in this book.

My goal is to save you the struggle – to present to you a view of God that is totally consistent with the Bible and with a rational, uncompromising view of modern science.

This is possible, because spirituality and science lie on two separate planes of thought. Things of the Spirit, of God, are not subjects for the laboratory simply because they cannot be observed. Science and the Scientific Method rely upon being able to observe the subject – Spirituality requires those non-quantitative disciplines of faith and belief in the unknowable.

As I see it there are 3 types of spiritual people in the world. There are those who believe, in some higher power, with all their heart. There are those who are convinced there is nothing and the majority, let's just call them "undecided" - who just aren't sure.

If you KNOW there is nothing – these words are not for you. Congratulations, if you have made peace with your beliefs and you are to be commended for your courage – however misplaced that may be. I will not seek to change your mindset; these words will mean nothing to you.

Just one thought about this in closing... how many things do we really KNOW for sure? Are you really SURE there is not a God?

A Note to Christians

For believers, you can accept or believe whatever you want, about certain "ancillary", that is non-core basic issues - as long as you believe the principles, nothing else really matters.

However, as an emissary of the Christian message it is very important what you say and how you present the plan of salvation to non-believers. Simplicity and consistency of message is paramount to their understanding of what is important. Do not infuse it with beliefs or conditions to belief that are not based on the Principles of Christianity. To do so, muddies the water and drives people away from understanding our Faith - thus we fail in our purpose.

Our Mission

Suppose that Christianity were a business (a big business) that generates billions of dollars in revenues from its followers.

Skeptics might argue that money and the power that goes with it, are the most important things to Christian leaders, as they surf their cable channels and stop for a few moments to amuse themselves reveling in the transparent hypocrisy of certain Televangelists or perhaps reading about corruption at the Vatican.

It is easy to forget that the Christian Religion, as represented by its churches, conventions, elders, leaders and spokespersons is only the human side of God's realm. Being human and run by humans, it is subject to err – for to err is human. This doesn't invalidate all that is done in the name of Christ, neither does it mean that all that is done by man in the name of God, is God's will and intent. Nor does it mean Christians are perfect.

In our humanness we fail to do things as they should be done and give fodder to our enemies who point to our failures as the punishment for hubris, hypocrisy and judgmental-ism. It is the patented Christian "better than thou" attitude that is misunderstood and vilified by the secular world – and for good reason!

Multitudes reject religion these days in favor of spirituality – meaning they want to reject that which is human and flawed in the business of modern religion and concentrate on the goodness of a Higher Spirit or Being. This is not all bad!

This doesn't for a moment, however, mean that we should just throw away organized religion, but it does mean that we should be more willing to accept it with all its flaws, as the best efforts of an imperfect species to understand our Maker. Nor does this mean that we should not strive for perfection in our institutions, just as God wants us to STRIVE for perfection in our personal lives. That we should fall short of both goals is understood.

How do we measure how we are doing with our collective efforts – to do this we must understand the goal.

The goal of Christianity, as dictated by our Founder – is measured by new subscribers to the faith. This is what is called the Great Commission – Christ's last words to mankind before he ascended to heaven. And like the last words of a man on his death bed, we must give great weight to what Christ chose has his last message.

He said, Go and tell others about me!

As a group, Christians seem to be doing everything possible to fail in this mission.

People can live for decades or an entire lifetime, even here in America - surrounded by Christian advocates, exposed to messages from Christian leaders in all forms of media - without understanding how or what to do to either accept or even reject the concept. Many don't even know the

basics principles of the Christian faith – and are surprised
when they discover the hidden secrets of faith!

For reasons that will be explored in this book – the
message is not getting through. Indeed, if Christianity
were a publicly traded business, our stock would be in the
dumps and shareholders would be clamoring for change.
Church attendance is down and people who identify
themselves as being "religious" are dwindling.
Denominations and churches struggle to stay relevant in a
world that has changed at the speed of light in the last 50
years. We have a huge branding and public relations
problem and our biggest enemy is ourselves.

Part of the problem is that we are such a fractured group,
that we have created over 41,000 different denominations
of Christianity – with each having a slightly different view
of some aspect of the Bible.

Some denominations think you should be sprinkled with
water and other immersed in Baptism, some believe that
you must add to what is in the scriptures by adopting
modern "messages" from God.

Others want to make Christianity a religion based upon
good deeds or the punishment of misdeeds, some want to
control behaviors through control their definition of sins
and others claim literal translations of the Bible are vital to
their faith. No wonder that non-Christians are confused

by a very fragmented message – who are Christians and what do they stand for?

Yet despite our 2,000 years of missteps, Christianity is one of the great religions of the world – with over 7 billion believers. In the United States over 70 percent of the population identify themselves as being Christian. Our success, you could say, is in the quality of our product and not in our stellar "sales and marketing"!

In spite of what seems like encouraging statistics; why is it that in the most pervasive religion in America, that so few people seem to "get it"? So many seem to be missing the point - In fact, few even know what is the real point of Christianity!

The reality of Christian, real Christianity as defined by Jesus himself, offers very little to "not like". Ours is a belief that is unlike any other religion on earth – it is based upon love alone. Christ said the greatest commandments are to love God and to love one another – if we do that, then everything else falls into place. Ours should not be a religion of Do's and Do not's – love is what drives you to Do or Do Not!

"Doing" without love gains you nothing in God's eyes – you cannot earn your way into His grace and into His heaven by your activities. Likewise, NOT doing certain things, will not get you closer to God either!

Christianity is based solely upon faith – faith in God and faith in His plan for your future and His forgiveness through your acceptance of his plan. Christianity, in fact, should be the ultimate Woodstock-type "HIPPIE" religion – founded and based in Love – offering hope, peace, tranquility and joy (maybe even music) to those who choose to believe.

Where is that message today? Ask the average "man (or woman) on the street" what they think it takes to be a Christian and you will get some very interesting answers.

I think it is high time to set the record straight - let us get right to the bottom line.

This is important!

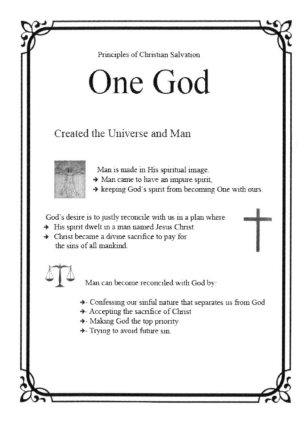

Forgive me if I repeat this!

This is Christianity in its simplest form – so simple, it is said, that even a Boomer can understand it!

- Why did it take over 30 years for this to sink into my head?
- Why do I hear from people, all too often, that they have lived their whole lives and have never understood this message?
- Why are there so many people who are confused by what is being said to them in the name of Christianity?
- Why do Christians of all denominations, put up roadblocks that hide this message?

The Bible

Let me explain my thoughts on the Bible overall:

As I have stated, I think the Bible has many levels – and has complexity that is elusive to many and some major mysteries that we may never understand.

On one level, the Bible is a History of the Jewish people. On another level it contains stories that explain, to the reader, the origin of earth and of man. On another level it gives a glimpse into the mind of God and His expectations for us. On yet another plane it explains God's plan for our reconciliation with Him, how God's spirit in the body of a man – lived his life, how and why he died and was separated from God for a time, how and why He was resurrected. Christians see references to the coming of Christ the messiah throughout the Old Testament.

And finally, there is prophecy; a great part of the Bible contains glimpses - hard to interpret and understand - of how our futures here on earth, and in heaven, are going to unfold.

The Bible contains parables, allegory, metaphor, historical facts and glimpses into the mind of God. It contains verses that should control your life and verses that, taken out of context or interpreted too literally, should not control your life! Knowing what to take to heart – or not – is part of the challenge when you read this rich document.

I would liken the Bible to one of the most complex human endeavors – a musical symphony! I'm no musician – trust me – but the complexity of such a composition, with its multiple movements, recurring themes, and multiple scores for a variety of instruments and for its beauty. Unlike a symphony composed by a human, the Bible is a work composed under the guidance and hand of God – by man. Even though, it was written by mankind, I believe the Bible as it exists today in any of its legitimate translations, says exactly what God intends for it to say to us.

Yet, having said this, understanding (true understanding) of the music of the Bible eludes many. This is consistent with what Christ told his followers when they asked him why he spoke in parables – and he said that it is not given to all people to be able to understand his message!

Here is an example of what this means; suppose you raise up a child, perhaps leaving the teaching of spiritual things until they could be properly and completely educated in the word of God. At the right, time you enroll that young person in, shall we say, a secular university for the study of religion – perhaps taking a course in Biblical Criticism.

Some, not all, institutions take the Bible and tear it apart – trying to find all that appears to be wrong with it. They are often successful because the Bible, composed by Man, is not a "perfect" document in all that it appears to be saying to us. This happens to the skeptical reader – of which I was once one – who tries to find out what is wrong with the Bible as opposed to the believing reader who seeks out the truth. Christians may refer to this as reading the Bible under the guidance of the spirit of God, and my experience tells me that this is the way to uncover the hidden layers of meaning, another movement – in the complex composition that is God's word.

Another round of ammunition for the skeptic comes when I said what the Bible "appears" to be telling us. I'm convinced that the Bible has some of the same "stumbling blocks" in it that Christ talked about, as impediments to understanding. Not all verses of the Bible are to be taken in their literal sense – just as what very little of what Christ spoke of was in the physical or literal sense, but in the spiritual sense.

There will be parts of the Bible that will confuse and trip up even the most-wise reader. This is why people report that they learn new things and gain fresh insight with each re-reading of the Bible or part thereof – this is true for me.

What is most revealing about the ability of mankind to understand and to interpret what is in the Bible is that there are over 41,000 CHRISTIAN DENOMINATIONS currently in existence!   If the truth were known to us, I believe that each person must read and understand and pray to receive divine guidance for understanding of God's word and how it applies to them. This would mean billions of denominations – since no two believers would have an identical understanding and experience in their relationship with God and God's word. To me, this is A-OK, since most of us would believe that the true essence of a God to human interaction is between the two parties and not for the interpretation and interference of another person or group.

One last caution! Avoid the trap contained in the statement, "To believe the Bible is to believe all the Bible – either you believe (every word literally of) the Bible or you don't!"

This implies that every single verse, must be taken in a superficial and isolated way – out of context, if you will. For example, the Bible forbids adultery. The same fundamentalist who says you must follow every word of the Bible, conveniently ignores Leviticus 20:10 which says "'if a man commits adultery with another man's wife--with the wife of his neighbor--both the adulterer and the adulteress are to be put to death."

Or perhaps we should follow the law in Leviticus 21:9 which proclaims that the daughter of a priest who is a prostitute should be burned to death?

There is at least one Christian pastor who is currently calling for the stoning of homosexuals.

The list of capital punishments goes on and on, of course, no one suggests that we should follow those laws today – we have used a higher level of understanding of the Bible to know that these types of laws are no longer applicable to us.

Many people, I suppose, would rather just have things spelled out for them; for it to be black or white with no nuances or shades – but it requires more than just a rote following of some written verses to serve a Master who wants us to dig into His word and come to an understanding of His intentions.

I believe that the Holy Spirit of God will lead the believer to understand the truth in His words. Conversely, those who read with the intention of disproving or finding what is wrong in the Bible will probably succeed.

One God

Sometimes I wish that the Bible didn't start with Genesis, but of course it does and must!

The story of creation and of the fall of mankind – is the first thing seekers must deal with when searching for answers and it is the first stumbling block. Talk about a formidable first task – and the confusion starts within the first 3 words – In the Beginning...!

There was a time, when believers were called upon to accept a literal translation of the book of Genesis and the creation story. People who disagreed with any of the ideas presented there, were labeled as heretics and sometimes burned at the stake. The early church not only held the literal to be true, but even added a bit of their own ideas that became sacred too – like the Earth was the center of the Universe. Even here in the 21st century there are religious leaders and followers who hold to the 7 day creation and all that goes with it.

The same people who must insist upon a literal interpretation of all that is in the book of Genesis and elsewhere in the Old Testament need to look a bit closer to the New Testament to gain an insight into the mind of God. As Christians we believe that Christ was "Emanuel" – God with us. I believe that Christ as a man who was filled with the spirit of God – he can give us some clarity into how God thinks!

Christ almost never spoke of the literal and physical part of things – and he was constantly misunderstood. We know of parables, of course, but also think about his thoughts about "living water", "bread of life" and being "born again" and many more metaphors. Even one of the most learned scholars of that time – Nicodemus wondered how a person could go back into the womb again!

The fact of the matter is – it doesn't really matter! In other words, this whole debate about the literal versus non-literal interpretation is tangential to the ideas in the basic Principles of Christian Salvation.

You, to be a Christian, can believe whatever your heart leads you to believe about anything else.

- If you want to think of God creating the world in 7 revolutions of the earth – then go for it!
- If you want to think that He planted fossils and in his infinite power and wisdom, just made it appear to us humans that the universe is billions of years old, then that is okay too.

Here is the problem with that approach however – it makes us less effective in our mission of bringing people to understand the Principles of Christianity!

The thing that is necessary to glean from parts of the book of Genesis is that there is a sovereign God and he, somehow, created or allowed the Universe to be created using the laws of Nature – either way works! In the same way, He created mankind, in this image – not PHYSICAL image – because God is not a man or a woman – but God is a spirit, an energy that pervades the entire Cosmos.

His dimension and being are outside of what we, as humans, are capable of understanding. He is outside of the scope of science, because science requires that we be able to OBSERVE the object being studied; to measure it, study it and record the findings. God is not observable to any scientific instrument ever devised and therefore and therein lies the conflict and confusion that the idea of God presents to the scientific community.

A prominent scientist has commented that God could not exist because intelligence requires a material substrate upon which it must exist – in other words, it requires a brain. This seems so near sighted to me! What about AI, for example. Artificial Intelligence (I'm NOT suggesting God is a computer or is AI by any means!) does not require a brain, but simply exists as energy that is applied to inanimate parts, created by humans.   It refutes the argument that intelligence requires a human-like brain.

I'm wondering then why it is much of a stretch to imagine that in all of the infinity of the Cosmos, that God might not have come to be – an intelligence that does not require the crude trappings of a perishable and earthly type body and a tiny brain, such as man does possess.

NOTE: I don't think God is a big computer!

What I do submit to the reader is that if we, with our tiny brains, can conceive of and construct a system that is intelligent and can learn to become even more intelligent, then why would not nature have developed this kind of power itself?

I see no reason why this would not have happened in all the eons of time and space – in fact I can see no other alternative that makes sense than that of an Intelligent Spirit or Energy that pervades and touches every fragment of the Cosmos.

Faith and not Works!

This is one of the most misunderstood aspects of Christianity!

Even people who have been Christians their whole lives miss this important point!

Suppose that you were God!

What kind of plan for reconciliation would you devise, for mankind? Parents, perhaps you even have a little background to help you with your task!

When you raise a child, you certainly must come to grips with controlling behaviors, punishment and reconciliation!   Perhaps you remember the terrible Twos, when a child begins to realize that it is an independent being and want to assert itself and even disobey you. At some point, you may have had to assert your authority, and to have punished the child for not obeying you. Perhaps at this point you were tempted to post a list of Do's and Don'ts – your version of the 10 Commandments. God too, tried a stop-gap plan of Laws; the 10 Commandments that were later translated into 613 laws by the Jewish people and then to over 40,000 customs and traditions that governed almost every activity of daily life.

Imagine, giving your child even 10 rules to follow – let alone hundreds or even thousands of instructions! What would happen if your child broke one of your rules? Would you then have to punish them? What punishment would you assign to the breaking of one of your rules? Are all transgressions the same to you or would you punish one type of transgression more than another?

In our imperfect world and imperfect example of comparing God's justice to that of an earthly father – keep in mind that we, as parents, do not administer our own system of justice in a fair and equitable way. Too often, we will just let things slide, a missed chore here and a surly remark there, overlooked until our tempers flare and we can lash out with a slap or by yelling or nagging our kids. Sometimes a favorite child is coddled, while the "problem child" is unfairly punished. Other times we punish the wrong thing, spilling some milk or breaking a glass by accident – instead of punishing a real offense such as disobedience.

I'm reminded of the scene from the movie "Kramer vs Kramer" when the boy Billy scoops up a big spoonful of ice cream, all the while ignoring his father, played by Dustin Hoffman, who is telling him to put the ice cream down. Despite all the warnings he takes a bit of the ice cream! The father carries the boy away to his room and when the boy says "I hate you!" the father replies "I hate you back, you little sh_t"! I always felt that the punishment of the boy would have been totally justified – as a perfect example of disobedience. Unfortunately, Hoffman's character, in all his humanity, makes a terrible error when he tells his son he hates him!

God makes no such mistakes; He never tells us he hates us and is always ready to forgive and forget when we ask, through our intermediary - Jesus. He always administers perfect justice by his very nature. Without some type of dispensation, each act of disobedience on our part would lead to punishment by God.

What is even more puzzling to many is the idea that, in God's eyes we are told, that all sin is equal and unacceptable. I agree that it is difficult to understand how, for example, greed or lust could be the same, to God, as murder or pedophilia! I think the answer lies in the very nature of God himself; tolerating only perfection – while at the same time – providing for a way for Him to overlook our humanly flaws.

What other system could there be?

How else could the imperfect be reconciled with the perfect?

We might imagine some other system as being more fair, such as some weighing of transgressions by the seriousness of the offense, like in our own judicial system.

In this scenario, murder and pedophilia, would carry the most severe sentence – while mere lust or greed or a disobedient bite of ice cream would be just a slap on the wrist – like a celestial parking ticket!

In this system, how many bites of ice cream would it take for God to punish us?   How much greed would be too much? How many murders would be OK?

This is clearly an unworkable plan!

God doesn't work this way – all sins are essentially disobedience to what God would have us do.

- o   Disobedience, without intermediation, is all punishable in the same way – eternal separation for the Goodness of Spirit that is God.
- o   Through what is called a New Covenant with mankind – God provided for us to be forgiven of our transgressions.
- o   With the forgiveness of God, no punishment is necessary.

About Sin

Christians have allowed the real message to be misplaced and corrupted. As I see it, the corruption of the message often comes from a focus on the manifestation of our human nature and imperfect belief and not on the underlying "disease" itself.

Let me tell you a story to illustrate my point.

Once there was a Doctor whose focus was upon treating his patient's symptoms. The Doctor was particularly focused upon reducing and eliminating fevers. When a patient would come to him, the very first thing he would do – in fact the only thing he would do - would be to take their temperature. If their temperature was too high, then he had many medicines and procedures to reduce the temperature back to a more normal range. If the patient's temperature was normal, then the Doctor would proclaim then healthy and send them on their way.

The Doctor never asked the patients if there was anything else bothering them; he didn't take their blood pressure or listen to their heart – to this not very good Doctor - temperature was the only important thing. Unfortunately, the Doctor seemed to lose a great many patients, because often the cause of the fever was due to a serious underlying cause – a disease. In many cases, the disease was treatable and if the Doctor had focused on treating the disease and not just focusing on the symptoms, many lives could have been saved.

In the same town lived a Preacher, who focused upon sin. Each week the Preacher focused upon a sin that was especially onerous to him.

One Sunday he would rail against thievery, the next he would condemn murder. He talked about how sinful it would be to break one of the 10 Commandments! He would strike fear into the congregation and was so effective in eliminating murder and theft that no one, to his knowledge, ever broke these laws.

But the Preacher spiritually "Lost" many Church members.

He lost them in a way that was more subtle that what the Doctor was experiencing – his people when they died were not saved, even though they never stole a thing.

They didn't understand their disease – lack of belief and faith in God - and instead they were living by the law. Just follow the rules and stay out of trouble. They missed the whole plan of salvation because they were not taught about the gift of Faith.

They were only focused on eliminating a sin in their life and not from understanding the underlying reason for unforgiven sin. We all sin and continue to sin – Christian or not – it is to be forgiven that is the key to salvation.

In the same way, what would we think about a Christian who wanted to focus on one symptom of our flawed human character?

How often do you hear Christians talking about, even condemning other people's behaviors?

No one is really safe from this Christian practitioner – non-believers and believers alike. There is a focus on the law or upon sin – (and it is someone else's sin that is under review – not their own.) Such as:

- o Thou shall not Dance!

The world calls it being judgmental and it is one of the distinguishing traits of us Christians. I certainly wish I could exclude myself from being a part of this group, but at times, I have been guilty of acting as a judge for someone else's behavior. Chances are you have done this too.

 Our Christian message becomes confusing to non-believers when we focus upon symptoms and not the disease. The average man or woman "on the street" would think that Christianity means NOT doing certain things – the message that is being sent is one of judgment and it's evil twin - hypocrisy.

We have set ourselves up for valid criticism through our "better than thou" attitude and turn countless people away from the real truth of Christ's sacrifice and God's forgiveness for our inevitable sins.

How about we stop and refocus on the Principles of

Salvation we have discussed?

Here is a modern day Parable to help you understand how Faith and your behavior might be intertwined:

Take two men, both are husbands.

One loves his wife and the other hates his wife.

The one who loves his wife, does things to show his love, to help make her life better, to be true to her and to honor her – because of his love he WANTS to do these things.

The other husband has a wife who has developed a set of rules for him to live by, since without them, he cannot behave in a way that is acceptable to her. The man often obeys his wife or shall we say he follows the rules – but not always – and when he does it is out of fear, expedience or habit, but because he does not love her, he is dreaming of the day that she may die or that he may be able to divorce her and find a new wife.

Which man best exemplifies what Christianity should be?

It is the loving husband, of course. Christ in his great wisdom told a young man the same thing – the most important "commandment" is Love! Love God and Love your fellow man. All the rest will then fall into place.

If the spirit of God is truly in your heart and soul – you, like the loving husband in our "parable" will WANT to do what is right.

Will you be perfect and always do what is the right thing? No! Even the apostle Paul, admitted that he couldn't do it, he couldn't be perfect – try as he would. So we certainly can't, and aren't, expected to achieve perfection either.

When (not if) we slip up – and when God is within us – we are forgiven for our trespass, because of our acceptance of his pardon through faith in his plan through the sacrifice of Jesus.

How about if we were to stop and refocus on the Principles of Salvation we have discussed?

About Repentance

Repentance is a journey not a destination. This was a great revelation for me! Christ said, "go and sin no more" to the prostitute and Paul said ... try as I might, I just cannot help but sin. How can we interpret these seemingly conflicting views?

They are not really in conflict – Christ says to her and to us "sin no more" and that *is* the standard and the goal for all mankind. That we must inevitably fall short of this comes as no surprise to God, but because of her belief in Christ and when we believe in Christ – we are no longer held accountable when we "mess up". So in God's eyes, the prostitute, through her belief in Christ, sinned no more – but was forgiven.

I was led to believe that my salvation was constantly in jeopardy, and that I was constantly need of a refreshing of my salvation every Sunday (and Wednesday nights too!). Heaven forbid that a truck should pull out in front of us on the way home and that our last words would be, "Damn". This swearing is surely a sin and that sin would condemn us forever to the fires of Hell – at least, according to the evangelists.

The fact is that no living being can just turn on a "Repent" switch and live a sin free life from that point forward –

notwithstanding the admonition of the robe-clad doomsday-er telling us to "Repent Now the End is Near!"

However, we can turn on a "In Process of Repentance" button, and should, as part of a belief in God. Here is how that would work for you.

First there is recognition that you are not perfect. Don't despair neither am I, or in fact any human on earth – you fit right in!

Since you are not perfect - you have sinned and you will sin again!

There are times when you haven't put God first in your life – when you have loved something, yourself or someone more than you loved God. Sure, we have all done this – it is our human nature at work. In fact, you may be one who doesn't even believe that a God is plausible, you have remained a skeptic – so putting God first would not even have been a consideration.

You are going to try very hard, in fact you are going to give it everything you've got, to remember God in what you do each day and even each minute in your life. Wait a minute you say, "Each Minute" – I don't think I can do that!

Of course not, if you could ... you would be perfect – but with God's help you will be surprised at how the ability to communicate with Him will grow and become part of your thoughts and consequently part of your actions. You will grow in your Faith and in your relationship with God as you strive for a connection with his spirit.

His plan meant that He himself would show us how we could try to live and in a sacrifice on our behalf, he gave up his earthly life and his soul for a time. His name was Jesus, or Emmanuel – meaning God among us – and He had the spirit of God within his humanly body.

Yet this becomes a stumbling block for many; including our children and grandchildren, friends and family members who think that first they must believe in the unbelievable face of God that mankind has created.

"I believe in the Big Bang"

"I believe in Evolution"

"I don't believe the Earth was created in 7 days"

"I don't believe that the Earth is only 6,000 years old"

"I don't believe that there was an Adam and an Eve (or Noah or Jonah)"

"I don't believe that Jesus was born of a virgin or came back to life"

"What about cavemen?"

"I don't think God is some old guy in white robes, up in the sky somewhere"

"Heaven, if there is such a thing, looks boring to me. Who wants to sit around on a cloud and play a harp all day long?"

"I believe in Science and not Religion"

"Religion is corrupt and full of hypocrites"

The Great Commission

And this is important because, it is our commission in life, as Christians, to tell the world about Christ – the only problem is that we are not doing a very good job.

Just to illustrate just how inept we really are as Christians there are estimated to be 41,000 different Christian denominations in the world!

How much must we quibble over the meaningless?

Things like: should you be completely immersed in water when you are baptized or is a sprinkle or two alright? Or do you even have to be baptized at all?

Apparently there are at least 41,000 ways to disagree as Christians – meanwhile the uninformed, the disenfranchised, the lost and hopeless remain untouched.

Instead let us focus on this:

Go therefore and make disciples of all the nations

Summary

Recently, I heard the testimony of a man, in his late 70's, who was being ordained as a deacon in my church.

A statement that he made startled me at first – he said that he was 70 years old when he first heard of God's plan for Salvation through Jesus Christ.

This might not be so unusual if this person lived in another country where Christianity was not the dominant religious view – but this man grew up in Northern California and lived much of his adult life in the Southeastern United States.

How can it be that this simple, basic message can be so muddled that even modern day Americans can go through their lives without ever hearing what it takes to be a Christian?

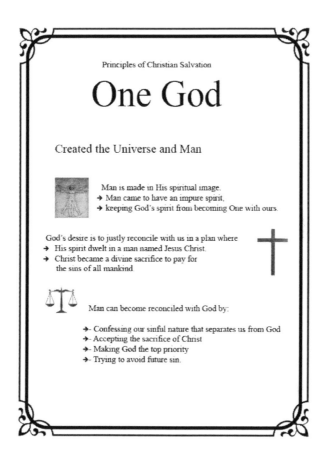

Principles of Christian Salvation

One God

Created the Universe and Man

Man is made in His spiritual image.
→ Man came to have an impure spirit,
→ keeping God's spirit from becoming One with ours.

God's desire is to justly reconcile with us in a plan where
→ His spirit dwelt in a man named Jesus Christ.
→ Christ became a divine sacrifice to pay for the sins of all mankind.

Man can become reconciled with God by:

→- Confessing our sinful nature that separates us from God
→- Accepting the sacrifice of Christ
→- Making God the top priority
→- Trying to avoid future sin.

Why are so many unbelievers confused?

How can we hone our message to eliminate the unimportant road blocks?

How can we do a better job of getting the word out?

This is our main job.

Who says?

Jesus Christ did - as He was ascending to Heaven.

His last words were ... "go tell others about Me."

Let us do our jobs to the best of our ability!

This is the time for Christians to refocus on telling the World this Good News by communicating the message of Jesus Christ in its purest and simplest form.

- No judgments
- No artificial roadblocks!
- Not by works or deeds

  but by Love and Faith!

Some of us never came home from Woodstock!

If you know a Boomer who is Lost and searching for answers, please tell them about this book and join us in our ministry by reaching out to another with a positive message of Hope.

Love God and Love one another!

Peace!

April 2015

Acknowledgements

Hubble photographs courtesy of STScI.

STScI is operated by the Association of Universities for research in Astronomy, Inc. under a contract with the National Aeronautics and Space Administration.